Sgaana Jaad ~ April White: Killer Whale Woman

The 25-Year Creative Journey of a Haida Woman as Represented Through Her Art

Dlunglas Kil'laagan,

Sgaana Jaad

April White

Edited by Judi Tyabji

First Edition
Maradadi Pacific, Powell River, Canada

Maradadi Pacific Holdings Ltd.

Powell River, BC, Canada

Cover art designed by Lens & Quill Designs with original artwork by April White. Book layout and photographs of April White by Lens & Quill Designs as commissioned by Maradadi Pacific.

All artwork in this book is from the collection of original paintings and serigraphs by April White.

Printing and binding by Friesens Corporation, Altona, Manitoba, Canada.

Canadian Cataloguing Publication Data

Tyabji, Judi, 1965 –

    Sgaana Jaad – April White, Killer Whale Woman

    Includes index

    ISBN 0-9809888-0-2

  1. Tyabji, Judi, 1965 - . 2. White, April, 1959 - . 3. Aboriginal Artists – Canada. 4. Haida Artists – Haida women. 5. Haida Legends and Art.
        6. Canadian Artists. 7. British Columbia Artists.

Table of Contents

Dedication

For G̲uud X̲angii, my Naani Daisy Edenshaw ~ Kwiyaa Jahlii, who gave me her spirit, and all who have given me their hands along my journey.

- A.W.

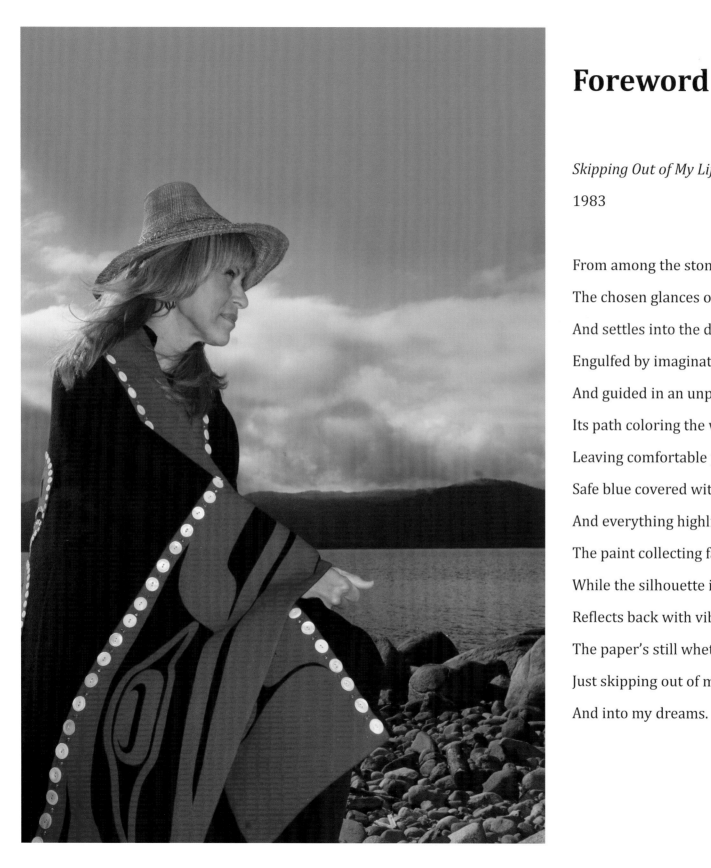

Foreword

Skipping Out of My Life, by April White

1983

From among the stones on the beach

The chosen glances over the water

And settles into the deep

Engulfed by imagination

And guided in an unpredictable direction

Its path coloring the world with sable brushes

Leaving comfortable pigments swirling with uncertainty

Safe blue covered with red laughter

And everything highlighted with adventure

The paint collecting faces in pools

While the silhouette in the changeroom mirror

Reflects back with vibrant orange

The paper's still whet.

Just skipping out of my life

And into my dreams.

About the Artist

Sgaana Jaad ~ April White, Yahgu'jaanaas Raven Clan

April White is an award-winning, internationally-celebrated artist whose work is on display in collections and galleries all over the world. She has been painting since the early 1980s and her art is represented in many museums. She was born on Haida Gwaii off the coast of northern British Columbia. Her father comes from a prominent family called Edenshaw, and she is descended from a line of powerful Haida chieftains. April's father and April's father's brother married two sisters; this double marriage ensured that April White is woven into the fabric of the Haida hierarchy and she has many cousins, aunts, and uncles in the Haida Gwaii region.

Her mother has a British-American background and April has been able to live in the Aboriginal and non-Aboriginal world throughout her life; sometimes she fits into both worlds and sometimes she feels removed from both as an outsider and an observer. Her unique perspective is that of a Haida woman who can also stand outside and look into the native world with a fresh view. This perspective molds the art and vision she presents in her paintings through her gentle, generous style.

April White can tell the stories of her home because she has lived so many of the lives of the characters in her paintings and travelled to so many remote parts of the land: she has celebrated with her clan at Potlatch ceremonies, she has worked on fish boats in the wild seas, explored the rocks and mountains as a geologist, journeyed to ancient villages to touch the totem poles of her ancestors, and walked on the beaches in storms. Through all of this her eyes, ears, and heart have been open to the whispers of the spirits of the forests, oceans, and open skies and her paint brush has brought this magic alive for us.

April White, a self-taught painter, has been inspired to paint hundreds of paintings over the years since her first paintings came alive in her mind and compelled her to leave her career as a geologist to become a full-time artist. Fifteen years ago she began screen printing, using this medium to define her growing need to explore Haida formline. For over twenty-five years she has populated galleries across North America and Europe and many of her paintings set a new standard of artistic expression.

In this presentation of April White's remarkable work we have selected from hundreds of original paintings and hand-pulled serigraphs and presented a wide representation of her art in four sections: Landscapes, the Haida World, Haida Spirits Manifest, and Haida Art and Legends.

The measure of an artist is represented by the body of his or her work and its resonance for those who encounter it. April White is truly a great artist in our time whose work will speak for many generations to come and tell the story of a strong, independent, ancient people and their land.

The Haida

The people indigenous to the islands off the northwest coast of British Columbia, known as Haida Gwaii, and some of the islands in the southern tip of the Alaska panhandle are known as the Haida. They are a fiercely independent people with a long proud history that is deeply entrenched in their customs, language, and culture. Knowledge is passed down through the spoken word and the elders apprentice the youth through the generations.

The Haida have lived in Haida Gwaii since time immemorial; they began their settlement on its exposed southern tip, and around 11,000 years ago, when the glaciers began to retreat, they expanded north. The abundance of food enhanced the development of a rich and dominant people with sophisticated crafts, culture and art. Their houses were immense, beams spanning their length, capable of housing thirty to fifty family members and entertaining two hundred during a potlatch. The Haida created strong sea-worthy red cedar canoes that took them as far as the north coast of California in raids to gather wealth and slaves. They became respected and feared along the coast of North America for their power, intelligence, and superior fighting and hunting abilities.

Before European contact it is estimated that there were 12,000 residents of the islands; some archeologists argue it could have been as high as 30,000 in the past. Disease decimated the population in the 1800s; currently there are approximately 7,000 Haida.

Today the Haida govern their land to protect their resources and their culture, negotiating agreements with the government of Canada, the government of British Columbia and private partners. Their culture has withstood decades of efforts to extinguish it. The embers of ancient knowledge and traditions were kept alive from within, and now through the synergistic effects of pride in self and a rich collective history, the people are rekindling their knowledge and traditions while gathering fuel to feed the fire that burns in celebration of the spirit of the Haida.

Haida Clan Structure

There are two primary clans that govern Haida relationships: the Ravens and the Eagles. Members of each group are assigned based on their mother's clan origin. Traditionally, when a Haida married it was to members outside their clan with the union arranged to gain alliances, to access natural and supernatural resources, and to establish higher social status.

In this moiety system, Ravens and Eagles are further subdivided into lineages, with offspring following a matrilineal succession. Of these subgroups, there were twenty-two for the Ravens and twenty-three for the Eagles. Historically, these clans were spread throughout the islands, comprised many households and even lived in separate villages.

Raven Visions
Original Watercolor, 2002
22" x 15"

Preeminent amongst the beings and oral history of the Haida, Raven, with his magical and supernatural powers, is primarily credited with transposing and transforming our shared universe to its present order. Raven is in the position of greatest importance on the totem pole, at the base. Looking seemingly straight ahead, Raven cocks his ear to listen for the call of Eagle.

Haida Gwaii – Islands of the People

The land of the Haida is remote, wild, and known for its ferocious weather. It is separated from the mainland of North America by Hecate Strait, a waterway that has the reputation of being the second most dangerous in the world. The first European explorers aptly named it after the Greek Goddess of destruction.

The islands of Haida Gwaii are heavily forested, with rocky cliffs, sandy beaches, and high mountains on the western ridge of the island chain. The mountain tops show the relatively recent glacial retreat. The islands are rich with marine life, clean air, pure water, transformational forests, and open beaches and bogs. There is a raw majesty to this place.

Ancient spirits are said to be apparent to sensitive visitors and the land is often called 'magic' by those who live there. A national park encompassing the southern islands, called Gwaii Haanas, defines the area as the 'islands of beauty and wonder'. Wildlife and sea life indigenous in this archipelago include a unique subspecies of black bear, otters, falcons, puffins, seals, sea lions, whales, salmon, halibut, starfish, clams, crab, hummingbirds, and of course, numerous ravens and eagles.

The largest stand of totem poles remaining in North America is on the remote southern edge of the park in a UNESCO world heritage site, where the remnants of ancient rainforest villages compelled Emily Carr to explore with her paint brushes. Her depictions distilled their essence and now bear witness to the rich heraldic past of the Haida.

April White's creative journey has drawn her home, to her birthplace on the edge of the earth, to Haida Gwaii. Inspiration was found along the way, but the heart of her soul lies in her paintings that tell the stories of her people.

ARCTIC
OCEAN

RUSSIA

GREENLAND

Bering
Sea

Gulf of Alaska

CANADA

Dixon Entrance

Kiusta

Naikoon
Hiellen
Old Massett

GRAHAM
ISLAND

*Hecate
Strait*

Skidegate
Queen Charlotte City

MORESBY
ISLAND

Gwaii Haanas
National Park Reserve

UNITED STATES OF AMERICA

ATLANTIC
OCEAN

*PACIFIC
OCEAN*

MEXICO

*PACIFIC
OCEAN*

Islands of the People
HAIDA GWAII

SGang Gwaay
Ninstints

Introduction

Hiking along the shore of Rennell Sound, a chance glimpse through a shroud of foliage and filtered golden light draws one in along the rock face, under the trees and into Haida Gwaii, the Islands of the People.

Come with us through the Secret Passage to explore the Natural Landscapes, The Haida World, Haida Spirits Manifest, and Haida Art and Legends through the eyes, paintbrushes and formlines of April White.

Secret Passage
Original Watercolor, 1993

Natural Landscapes

The Path

Original Watercolor, 2007
22" x 30"

Pause, draw in moist air, give in to the surrounding moment and be absorbed. Reflect on sunlight as it gently tumbles through Trees' outstretched arms and softly emanates from contented Moss. As the mind slips from the immediate and rolls forward, take a step and follow the red trodden carpet. Find serene exhilaration along the path through an ever-evolving rainforest.

Footprints in the Sand

Original Watercolor, 1988
22" x 30"

The fine sand is moved by the wind, forming soft dunes on the north coast of Graham Island in Haida Gwaii, the remote islands off the northern west coast of Canada. The dunes part to form a path west of Yakan Point, drawing one in for a walk on the beach.

A Knotty View

Original Watercolor, 1988
22" x 30"

For a 'knotty view' kneel to peek through the keyhole to see life on the other side. Look closely and you will see the beauty that looks back and defies the rough exterior that frames the vision.

Snag's Apprentices

Original Watercolor, 1993
30" x 22"

Snag is a being that lives in the Tsim-shian's Skeena River country and is a Raven crest. He can assume different forms. Here he is teacher and classroom, as he holds the young apprentices high in the sky to hone their keen vision and to learn that with the power of obser-vation and attentive patience, comes opportunity.

Through the Pier

Original Watercolor, 1993
40" x 30"

The derelict pilings and the underside of the pier at the end of Nadu Road frame Massett Inlet in a tranquil moment that belies the fast six-to-seven knot current that courses in and out with each tide. On the shore an alder tree stoops as its branches seemingly reach to pick up the rare fire agates amongst the ordinary grey stones .

Across the Hiellen

Original Watercolor, 1993
29 1/2" x 41"

The base of Tow Hill in Haida Gwaii provides the vantage point for this view across the Hiellen River mouth to North Beach. The sand stretches to Naikoon (long nose) in the distance where Raven, according to Haida legend, hearing noises in the clam shell and compelled by curiosity, investigated. He prised open the shell releasing what was inside, miniature human beings, who quickly fled to the forest beyond. These first people are the ancestors of the Haida.

Rocks in the Mist

Original Watercolour, 1992
15" x 22"

The vision ahead and beside, in the chance passing on a fishing vessel, is captured with a wisp of pigment and water. The mist is like a veil hanging from a bed canopy, softening to an apparition what is behind; the sea gently caresses the rocks of the shore and stretches to reflect the entwined branches of resting trees.

Hippa Fangs

Original Watercolor, 1984
22" x 30"

The mystical rocks on the west cost of Haida Gwaii are exposed to the open sea and their ominous look serves as a warning to those on the ocean looking for safe harbor. According to some legends, one of the key pillars of Hippa Fangs is cursed and one can see this because no gulls will land there and the rocks are barren.

Room with a View

Hand-pulled serigraph with watercolor, 1997
13 1/2" x 21 1/2"

Impenetrable walls leave shoulders cloaked in black as you turn to watch the light. The light waltzes with the clouds, skips across the water, hops along the rocks like a raven, frolics through the trees, and tiptoes across the sand to reach the room with a view.

Foam Woman

Original Watercolor, 1993
15" x 22"

Emerging from the foam created from fresh river water, tumbling seas and whipping winds is the spirit of foam woman. Seeing her face in profile masks her tremendous power; she warns with a wink and can hold a supernatural being at bay with just a look from her eyes.

The Raven lineage came from the womb of Foam Woman. At her numerous breasts, as many as ten on each side, she nursed a grandmother from each of the Raven families among the Haida.

The Haida World

Edenshaw Potlatch Dancer

Original Watercolor, 2000
29 1/2" x 41"

Chilkat colors cloak a young Eagle dancer as he takes flight to celebrate the gathering of Haida and their honored guests in the traditional Haida Potlatch ceremony. Here, both the Raven and Eagle clans come together to memorialize the Chief's passing, and to bear witness as the next Eagle Chief of the Stastas Songcloth Clan takes the hereditary name, Edenshaw (ᚒIDansuu).

It is believed that the more lavish the celebration, the more likely it will be that these stories will be remembered. Thus, oral history is passed from generation to generation.

Hearing Aid by Bear Cub

Acrylic on canvas, 2000
16" x 20"

With toed paws flexed, eyes inquisitive, ears forward, and hind legs anchored through the ears of Grizzly who is below him, Bear Cub is on the alert! He is ready to respond to the slightest sound as the huge Bear's hearing aid.

A Raven Clan crest, Bear is known for his superior senses and is often depicted with prominent eyes, ears, nostrils and tongue.

Wealth in Song

Acrylic on Canvas, 1998
16" x 20"

Music and song have always been woven through Haida daily life: weft of baby lullaby and on through mourning, warp of potlatch and on through warfare, weaving the vessel to carry the culture and the history of a people. Without a history of written language, the art of the oral tradition is a living and evolving entity preserving the cultural wealth of the people through songs and poetry.

The songs are owned and passed down through the family lineage and is a key part of any Haida's inheritance. Permission to sing another's song can only be granted by the owner.

A Haida Elder in song defines the wealth of this nation.

Urban Legend

Original Watercolor, 2008
29¹/₂" x 41"

White Raven is a supernatural being with powers to transpose and transform and a genius for trickery. Chance puts Raven at the entrance to his Grandfather's house. He is asked to fetch a box within a box which has two pebbles; one white and encrusted with crystals and the other black. These, the Chief instructed with their giving, were to create land. On the first try, Raven failed by doing things backwards. The second time he created the mainland out of the white pebble and Haida Gwaii out of the black pebble.

With the extreme confidence that comes with being a principal player in the ordering of the universe, White Raven travels through time to the present and swaggers down the dangerous divide, again with an eye to opportunity. Walking down the transition between two worlds he could stumble upon a stepping stone to open the cosmos for the rest of us.

Gift of Hands

Original Watercolor, 2007
15" x 11"

Looking out from beneath the beak and embraced by the protective wing of Eagle is Human. What sets this Being apart from all the others in this world are his hands.

The word stlanlaas translates as 'good with their hands'. This is the closest equivalent in the Haida language to the honored calling of Artist.

The renowned Haida artist and Stastas Eagle Chief, Charles Edenshaw, when asked what he would like to leave his heirs replied, "my hands".

In the Beginning

Original Watercolor, 2002
41" x 29 1/2"

In the beginning, Raven (Yaahl) wore a cloak of white feathers. This Raven, who alone of his kind survived the Great Flood, was not an ordinary bird: he brought the First People and the Light into this world. Raven carried the sun, the moon, and the stars to the outside world through the smokehole of a great Chief's longhouse. This route of escape has great mythical significance, as it is held to be the reason his feathers became black.

In the beginning, fireweed covers the land, heralding the regeneration of the forest.

In the beginning, a juvenile Raven, represented in its primal form by this young Raven dancer, carries the future of the people, the Haida.

Three Watchmen

Original Watercolor, 2007
15" x 11"

Only the greatest of Haida chiefs had Three Watchmen with high hats carved at the top of their longhouse frontal poles. The Three Watchmen sit high above the rooftops in constant vigil, with one looking straight ahead to the horizon and the other two scanning the shoreline as it stretches out from their community to a distant shore.

These human figures represent actual watchmen who were stationed at strategic lookouts to alert the village of anyone approaching, whether family, friend or foe.

Emerging Frog

Original Watercolor, 1999
22" x 15"

The traditional Haida homes have interior poles to hold up the roof and keep the building strong. It is said that the Haida carve a frog on one of their house poles to prevent the building from toppling over.

Frog is shown here emerging from the mouth of bear. This oft-depicted bearer of good luck can be recognized by its wide mouth, thick lips and bulging eyes. Signs of the ancient traditions can be seen in the sites of the old villages in Haida Gwaii.

Bear Spirit

Original Watercolor, 1998
41" x 29¹/²"

The Bear's superior strength and senses makes it not only an exceptionally powerful animal but a spirit being that is higher than all others. The Native people of the northwest coast claim Bear for one of their crests and tales of Bear appear throughout Aboriginal mythology.

Eaglet's First Flight

Original Watercolor, 2001
41" x 29¹ᐟ²"

The Haida and their honored guests gather on Haida Gwaii for the Hereditary Chieftainship Potlatch where an Eagle will take on the name Edenshaw.

In performance for the new Chief, a Haida Eaglet dons the ceremonial regalia of his clan. Apprehensive, but surrounded by his family and his people, he looks forward to his first flight.

He is the future.

Haida Spirits Manifest

Sgaana ~ Killer Whale

Original Watercolor, 1986
30" x 40"

In the Haida cosmos, the souls of animals are considered the same as the human soul. They have their own territories, villages, and similar hierarchy. In their homes, their form is human and upon leaving they don cloaks and masks and speak as the animal.

The Killer Whale with a hunter on its back breaks the barrier between the two worlds. Under the sea exists the lower world which is the realm of the Killer Whale People. In ceremony and ritual, wearing the animal's cloaks and masks, mimicking their voices and movements, one enters and becomes part of the Animal's society.

Raven Steals the Light

Hand-pulled serigraph with watercolor, 1997
10" x 28"

In Haida legend, there was a time when the whole universe was black. All light was hidden in the Sky Chief's longhouse within a box, which the trickster Raven decided to steal. Pursued by Eagle he fled, spilling pieces of light that became our stars. As he passed the edge of the world, Raven flung the last shards of light, which floated down gently to touch the clouds and became the sunset.

Koyah and the Keeper of the Moon

Original Watercolor, 1998
41" x 29 1/2"

With every turning of the Moon, the Keeper tantalizes Raven with glimpses of Raven's coveted prize. The Moon's actions cause the tides, which ebb to reveal the rich feasts on the beaches: clams, crab, seaweed and octopus. The Moon gives light for man to fish at night.

The Keeper vigilantly counters Raven the trickster's every move, preventing Raven from stealing the Moon. The Keeper knows that the Moon's illuminating of the darkness, and ebb and flow of the tide eases man's journey through life.

Metamorphosis

Original Watercolor, 2005
41" x 29 1/2"

Raven must search for a land that holds a new beginning. He sets out with Butterfly as companion and escort. Acting as scout, Butterfly ascends high above the earth's surface looking for good land which he points out with his uncurled proboscis. He tells Raven that choosing a gwaii or islands where bears live is a good idea since this land will be plentiful in salmon and berries. The wondrous place they found through this search became Haida Gwaii, the Islands of the People.

Butterfly's spiritual metamorphosis within the cycle of life begins by landing on a salmonberry flower.

Balance

Hand-pulled serigraph, 1994
13 3/4 x 19 3/4

Balance Rock is a glacial erratic deposited upon a shale beach on Haida Gwaii. It has borne witness to 10,000 years of pounding waves from Hecate Strait.

The Haida spirit that manifests through Balance Rock shows Thunderbird Moon who looks to the future and the human infant form at the point of equilibrium symbolizing the balance between Eagle and Raven, the two clans of the Haida Nation.

"BALANCE"

April White
1994

Whale Play

Original Watercolor, 1995
41" x 29 1/2"

A killer whale raises its tail in play, silhouetted by the last light of a summer's evening. The reflection in the gentle ocean interprets that motion, in perfect synchronicity through the graphic imagery of the Northwest Coastal peoples.

K'iid K'iyaas
The Golden Spruce

Watercolor original, 2007
30" x 22"

The story of K'iid K'iyaas (Ancient Tree) begins in a village at the headwaters of the Yakoun River, known as the River of Life. The people, well-provisioned by the river's bounty, became arrogant and began to fight. This disrespect for the river's gifts brought a time of unrelenting snow. Unable to replenish their winter stores and firewood, the villagers began to die of starvation and cold. Only an old man and his grandson survived and escaped to the forest where it was summer. As they journeyed downriver in search of a new home, Tsinni the grandfather warned the boy, "Don't look back. If you do, you will slip into the next world." Overwhelmed with nostalgia, the boy glanced back and his feet became rooted to the forest floor. He grew into the supernatural spruce tree with needles of gold. His grandfather sadly left him with these parting words, "When you grow old and fall, your fallen body will become a nurse log and you will rise up again, standing until the end of the world. Each generation will look to you and remember your story." Since then, the Golden Spruce summons the Sun to illuminate his needles so he can pass on his message to respect the wisdom of the Elders.

Salty Isle's Otter

Hand-pulled serigraph with watercolor, 2006
8 ³/₄" x 13"

Sea Otter safely enjoys an evening meal of a mollusk garnered from the deep. Vulnerable while using his chest as a table, he finds protection in the obscuring shadow of the weather-beaten vessel Salty Isle, while the ocean's ripples in formline disguise his silhouette.

Once abundant along the Pacific Northwest Coast otters were hunted to near extinction by the mid-1800's for their uniquely exquisite fur. A lifetime spent swimming in the ocean's cool water results in a fine and dense protective fur, impregnable to water and life-taking cold.

Otter came into the world with a long, spear shaped tail through an encounter between the mischievous Raven and a man attempting to pre-empt Raven's propensity for transforming humans into animals. Preparing to slay the trickster with a sharp spear, man was transformed, spear and all, into Otter.

Haida Warrior

Hand-pulled serigraph, 1995
7" x 10 1/4"

Designed by April White's grandfather Geoffrey White of Old Masset in Haida Gwaii, and built by Geoffrey White, his sons and Andrew York, the seiner Haida Warrior runs on its maiden voyage to Prince Rupert.

Ahead of its wake, the Eagle Spirit, which represents Geoffrey's son Oliver White, will always be a guide to safe harbor for fishing vessels in peril.

Supernatural Beings

Original Watercolor, 2005
22" x 30"

Before the arrival of Humans, the world was inhabited only by Supernatural Beings.

Killer Whale Sgaana is the most powerful of all the Ocean Peoples. The Sgaana have a complex society where they commune in underwater villages and assume the human form. While hunting or travelling they are supreme in their world; strong and sleek, transformed to Killer Whales.

Thunderbird Hiilaang resides high in the mountains, also in human form, and when hungry, cloaks himself in feathers to create wings. Taking to flight in his search for food, his body is of such enormous size that he darkens the sky. We hear the clap of his wings as thunder and see the flash of his tongue as lightning.

Stooping with great velocity Hiilaang plunges towards Sgaana and grips his back with his deadly talons.

One senses the power of these Supernatural Beings as they collide at the intersection of their separate worlds, the surface of the great ocean.

The Artist ~ On a Watermelon Blanket

Original Watercolor, 1989
30" x 40"

The artist sits on a watermelon blanket, with arms drawing knees tightly to her breast, on South Beach, northern Haida Gwaii. Her mind drifts to the ancients and transforms her while she is bathing in the sun's warming, cleansing and nurturing light.

As she slips back to the present, words become the pigment that settles and absorbs into the paper. Next, the multiple layering of color forms connection, and then the detailing of grammar gives the dimension for sharing her experience in words.

Haida Art and Legends

White Raven's Moonlit Flight

Hand-pulled serigraph, 2000
16" x 22"

Through his power as the Transformer and his use of trickery, Raven stole the Moon from the Chief of the Haida. Flying with it over the Nass River, he came upon eulachon fishermen. Raven, being hungry, said, "If you will give me eulachon, I will give you light to fish by in the darkness." In disbelief, they watched as Raven revealed the Moon, and they were able to fish by its light. Grateful for this gift, they gave him his fill of this prized fish.

Seeing no further use for the Moon, Raven flew away and tossed it into the dark sky.

Raven Star I

Hand-pulled serigraph, 2005
11" x 10"

Disguised as Sea Star with radiating arms, Raven, the legendary transformer, spreads his wings, tail and beak outwards. Circles as tube feet and salmon heads at the ready for a meal, there awaits the connection with human hand and inquisitive mind. In Haida myth form, during Raven's swift retreat from Great Chief's Longhouse with all the Light in his beak, his prize begins to fragment, falls and strikes the earth. Most splinters ricochet out of the blackness becoming stars; some are claimed by the ocean's waves and appear as sea stars.

As we bend down to see we begin to understand the world around us and through this can begin to fathom the depths and the heavens in our never ending quest for knowledge.

Eagle IV

Hand-pulled serigraph, 2005
11³/₈" x 8"

Guud (Northern Bald Eagle) is a member of the Accipitridae Clan and in both name and stylized image has represented one of the moieties of the Haida since these families "first came out" from Property - Making - a – Noise - House. Eagle's relatively short beak terminating in a strong down-ward curve, contrasting white head and tail, and chittering vocalizations assures its recognition. The constant search for sustenance results in the fleeting satisfaction of a relished salmon head filling its belly.

The eaglets, depicted in the wings, are raised in a refurbished nest that is straining its perch atop a tall tree. A Haida Eagle Chief will welcome all to a Feast by commanding a dance that disperses Eagle Down into the air, allowing this symbol of peace and friend-ship to gently float and settle on everyone.

Sgaana IV

Hand-pulled serigraph, 2001
11 3/8" x 8"

Sgaana, in the Haida language, represents both Killer Whale and Power. The power of Killer Whale is dual: the head is masculine, fierce, seemingly omnipotent, while this supernatural being's supreme strength is balanced by the feminine Jaad depicted in its tail. Thus, strength is balanced through fluid grace.

The sun in this depiction is a visual homonym as both life-giving rays of light and life-supporting ribs. When Raven steals the light and inadvertently shares it with the world, the Village of the Whales lying under the sea is also affected. The sun's rays become a part of the Whale's domain either by reflection or by penetration of the surface to their undersea world.

Hummingbird I

Hand-pulled serigraph, 2006
7 1/2" x 11"

Dakdakiiyaa (Hummingbird) is a member of the Trochilidae Clan and in Northwest Coast imagery is recognizable by its long slender beak and outspread wings, ready for flight. This latter characteristic emphasizes its unique ability to fly in any direction. Indeed, this phenomenon, signaled by a musical buzz and iridescent flash and blur, facilitates its supernatural travel between human world and spirit world.

In this depiction, a naked hatchling is sheltered under its mother's wing with mouth agape in expectation of a sweet meal. This repast of nectar has been gathered from the throats of hundreds or thousands of flowers then whisked to the nest at the forest edge to a home insulated with moss, lichen, down and spider webs.

Once the traditional order of Haida matrilineal succession was jeopardized by the capture of a high-born Haida Eagle Clan woman at Lax Kw'alaams (Port Simpson). This order was restored by the delivery of her children home to Haida Gwaii with the gift of the Hummingbird as a new family crest.

Raven II

Hand-pulled serigraph, 2005
11" x 7 1/2"

Yaahl, alias Raven, is the trickster cousin in the Corvidae Clan. Raven is motivated by insatiable desires to legendary antics, and is the most important of all creatures on the Northwest Coast. As a clan symbol it identifies half the Haida society, and as a crest, is claimed by all Haida people. Full of magical powers, this supernatural being, with its sleek black lines, thick straight beak and prominent 'ears', is the transformer-creator principally responsible for changing the world to its present form.

An opportunistic forager, Raven now feasts on both crab and a salmon head which he shares with his fledgling young. In the shelter of parental wing feathers, these new lives open their mouths with expectation.

Tufted Puffin III

Hand-pulled serigraph, 2004
11 x 7 $^{1/2}$"

Tufted Puffin, of the Alcidae Clan, is an easily recognized inhabitant of the Pacific Northwest with a stubby black body, white face, tufts of long feathers behind his eyes and a large orange parrot-like bill. Short narrow wings serve both in diving deeply and flying swiftly, and the large webbed red feet can double as brakes. Puffin live in colonies that are situated on vertical sea cliffs and on a diet of small fish.

This depiction shows the chick tucked into the wing. The chicks are raised on the catch delivered to the nest site in the adult bird's large bill. The usually silent parent uses protective growling notes to communicate when home in the nest.

Puffin beaks, gathered after their annual moulting, were prized by the Haida for their use in ceremonial regalia.

Chíin Xaadee ~ Salmon People I

Hand-pulled serigraph, 2007
11" x 22"

The indigenous peoples of the Northwest Coast are salmon people. Each species of salmon, with its seasonal order of appearance, dictated human activities, and indeed their wealth. Historically, the sea's bounty was so great and easily harvested that the Northwest Coast had one of the densest non-agricultural human populations on earth. These resources freed time to develop a highly complex culture.

This is a formline depiction of a spawning female and male Oncorynchus tshawytscha, known commonly by various names: Chinook, Spring, King, Tyee, Blackmouth, and in the Haida language, Taawaan. They are the largest of all the Pacific salmon, and being anadromous, hatch in freshwater, spending time in estuaries and shorelines before going to sea, then returning to their birthplace stream to spawn anywhere from their second to seventh year.

Travel in the freshwater spawning migration can be extensive; up to two thousand river miles over a sixty-day period. The human figures within the design signify the valuable role salmon play in our lives and our need to honor and respect this relationship.

Blue Heron IV

Hand-pulled serigraph, 2005
14" x 8"

Great Blue Heron, a member of the Ardeidae Clan, is easily recognizable by his long slender blue-grey form. Standing nearly motionless though gliding gracefully forward, Hlguu iiwans' silhouette, heightened by evening's falling light, is an intimate apparition as he silently stalks in the shallows. Heron's eyes are intent on divining underwater, through the shimmer of reflected light and every life-inspired ripple, the signal that will trigger a swift snatch of fish or eels from the water.

The proclamation of success appears as meals of eels sliding down paralleling sinuous lines. Sheltering under the parent's wing, the naked hatchling is seen, satisfied with a full belly. This is the reward for a twenty to thirty mile flight to forage, sustaining new life. Paramount is another generation to teach, for in Haida mythology, the Heron appears as an industrious old man, Stlanlaas, who is good with his hands and a master at carpentry and art.

Bear Mother Myth I

Hand-pulled serigraph, 2003
22 1/4" x 11 1/2"

As told in the Bear Mother Myth, the beautiful young daughter of a Chief was out berry picking and neglected to perform the traditional singing to warn the Bears of human presence. This lack of respect for the Bears causes her abduction by the Prince of the Bear People. Her high rank forces their marriage, but relentless pursuit by her brothers to find the lost Princess causes the Bear Prince to flee with her. He hides her high in a tree on a mountain, where she gives birth to twin bear cubs.

Ultimately, she and the Prince of the Bear People are both found. As Bear prepares for death he removes the cubs' bear garments, transforming them into human beings, pre-destined, like the Bear, to become the greatest of hunters. In this depiction, the Bear Prince is in constant vigil with the Human mother in his shoulder and two cubs below.

Summer Solstice

Hand-pulled serigraph, 2003
22" x 22"

Central to the North's cosmos is Juuyee (Sun) as it inexorably shares never-ending light during Summer Solstice. Under this nurturing light is the remote archipelago of Haida Gwaii, home to the Haida. Here all Haida people announce themselves as either Raven or Eagle.

This mandala, representing a microcosm of life, focuses embryonic light to shared vision. Primary to this, Raven the Creator is in his solitary orbit questioning, challenging and learning. Next, concentric but in an opposite direction is Eagle searching, soaring and seeing. Enveloping all through transposition are both birds circling on the same plane in perfect synchronicity.

This harmonious union is a celestial embrace for all to see and is cause for celebration.

June 21st 2003 Summer Solstice

Acknowledgements

This book is the culmination of twenty-five years of April White's hard work and inspiration that yielded the hundreds of magic paintings and serigraphs now hanging in galleries, institutions, and private collections all over the world. The Haida legends and stories that accompany much of the art were compiled by April White over her years of research into the sources of her inspiration. These legends have evolved through the centuries and have been handed down through the oral traditions of the Haida. Variations of these stories will be found in other sources.

It is not the intent of this book to provide a definitive reference on the Haida people, their legends, history or culture. Hopefully what you encounter in this book will motivate you to seek out other sources and learn more about the fascinating background, stories, and culture of the Haida and the Haida Gwaii region.

This book would not be possible without the dedication of people who helped make it happen including Emma Levez Larocque, Katie McLean, Kathy Thomson, Mischa Brooks-Thoma, Marlane Christensen and others and without the support of Gordon Wilson, partner in Maradadi Pacific.

Index

Artist April White in traditional Haida button blanket holds one of her Argillite creations.